Benjamin Relyea

The nation's mourning

A sermon, preached before the Congregational Church and Society in

Green's Farms

Benjamin Relyea

The nation's mourning
A sermon, preached before the Congregational Church and Society in Green's Farms

ISBN/EAN: 9783337112936

Printed in Europe, USA, Canada, Australia, Japan

Cover: Foto ©Lupo / pixelio.de

More available books at **www.hansebooks.com**

THE NATION'S MOURNING.

A

SERMON,

PREACHED BEFORE THE

CONGREGATIONAL CHURCH AND SOCIETY IN GREEN'S FARMS, CONN.
ON THE DAY OF THE NATIONAL FAST,

OCCASIONED BY THE DEATH

OF

ABRAHAM LINCOLN,

President of the United States,

JUNE 1st, 1865.

By REV. B. J. RELYEA.

PASTOR.

New York:

JNO. P. PRALL, PRINTER BY STEAM, No. 9 SPRUCE-STREET.

1865.

A

SERMON,

PREACHED BEFORE THE

CONGREGATIONAL CHURCH AND SOCIETY IN GREEN'S FARMS, CONN.,
ON THE DAY OF THE NATIONAL FAST,

OCCASIONED BY THE DEATH

OF

ABRAHAM LINCOLN,

President of the United States,

JUNE 1st, 1865.

By REV. B. J. RELYEA,

PASTOR.

New York:

JNO. P. PRALL, PRINTER BY STEAM, No. 9 SPRUCE-STREET.

1865.

CORRESPONDENCE.

GREEN'S FARMS, June 5th, 1865.

Rev. Mr. RELYEA,—

Dear Sir: In accordance with the general and often repeated wish of your congregation, on Fast Day, we would respectfully request the publication of your sermon, delivered on that occasion. We believe it to be timely, instructive, well fitted to be useful, and well worthy of permanent preservation.

Yours affectionately,

E. B. ADAMS.
JOHN S. HYDE.
E. J. TAYLOR.
S. B. SHERWOOD.
JARVIS JENNINGS.
H. B. WAKEMAN.
J. B. ELWOOD.
T. B. WAKEMAN.
DANIEL BURR.
F. SUMNER.

REPLY.

GREEN'S FARMS, June 7th, 1865.

DEACON E. B. ADAMS AND OTHERS,—

Gentlemen:

Your note of the 5th inst. has been handed to me. The sermon to which you refer, was written hastily in the ordinary course of preparation for the pulpit, without the remotest thought of its being published. My individual preference would lead me to decline giving it to the public in the form you suggest; but I find it difficult to refuse compliance with the request of a people from whom so many tokens of kindness have been received. I therefore place it at your disposal, and you are at liberty to make such use of it as you may think proper. In doing so, I have the satisfaction of feeling fully assured that it contains no sentiments but such as are held in common by the members of this society, who though in some respects they may differ in political sentiments, yet have had enough of good sense to maintain harmony among themselves, and enough of patriotism not to shrink from their full share of the burdens and sacrifices necessary to preserve unimpaired the authority of our national government.

Very sincerely, and with much esteem, yours,

B. J. RELYEA.

SERMON.

" And all Judah and Jerusalem mourned for Josiah."

II Chron. xxxv. 24.

In every great bereavement, whether individual or national, the benefit to be derived results not from the first ebulition of painful and sorrowful feeling, but from the subduing influence of after reflection. In the first moments of grief our minds are filled with a tumult of emotions which renders us for the time incapable of fully comprehending the meaning of the event—of measuring the interests affected by it, or of learning the lessons which it teaches. It is only when time and nature have come to the aid of reason, and given calmness to our minds, that we are able to indulge in such meditations as shall suitably impress the heart and influence the life.

It is eminently appropriate, therefore, that such a day as this should have been set apart in view of that event which has filled the nation's heart with sorrow; and it is well that it should have been deferred to this distance of time. The first bewilderment of the sudden and stunning blow—the tumult of excited and conflicting emotions which struggled in the national mind—the roll of muffled drums—the tolling of bells—the solemn tramp of civic and military processions, with all the pomp and pageantry of a nation's woe, have passed away. And we shall be able perhaps more calmly to view the bereavement and to consider the lessons which it teaches.

The most striking and showy demonstrations of grief are not always indicative of deepest and most lasting sorrow. I have learned seriously to doubt the depth and sincerity of the man's real, self-denying patriotism, who finds it necessary to be always giving some marked proof or protestation of his loyalty. I put such an one down as having either a soft head or an unsound heart. So in the case of national bereavement. It is not the most ostentatious display of grief that is always most genuine. Great depth of feeling is not apt to be over demonstrative. Deep waters flow with a comparatively calm and quiet surface. Shallow streams are always most boisterous. When a man is found babbling of his own great sorrow, and lamenting the want of it in others, generally you do not greatly err in esteeming him to be one of those shallow streams —a man whose feelings lie very much on the surface, and not likely to be greatly benefitted by the affliction.

Neither is it true that the first outburst of uncontrollable feeling, however real, is always followed by that permanent improvement of character without which affliction fails to accomplish its end. You have sometimes witnessed instances of individual or family bereavement, in which the first tumult of emotion seemed for the time ungovernable ; yet in the course of a few months, or even weeks, the whole current of their thoughts and of their lives was as vain and frivolous as if no such affliction had befallen them. You have witnessed other instances of affliction borne with comparative serenity, and with little outward demonstration, which has, nevertheless, left its mellowing and subduing influence upon the whole after life. Thus in national bereavement. While a solemn and becoming respect for the nation's dead, and a suitable regard for the forms and manifestations of sadness are always eminently fit and proper, it is well to remember that true sorrow does not consist in the trappings and decorations of mourning, but in a heart contrite and bowed down with grief. The benefits of affliction are not derived from transient feeling, however violent, but from calm reflection, and the abiding, deep-toned impression left upon the mind.

It is evident, from the following history, that the general mourning of the Jewish nation, on the occasion referred to in the text, partook very much of this ostentatious and evanescent haracter—that it was not accompanied by repentance of heart, nor followed by any lasting improvement in their way of life.

On the death of Josiah there was indeed occasion for great lamentation and mourning. More than people at the time were aware of. He was a man of extraordinary virtue and piety. He shone as a star of the purest lustre in a corrupt and degenerate age. Soon after he had ascended the throne he set about the reformation of manners and religion. He destroyed idolatry throughout the land. He brake down their idols and their altars, and defiled them with dead men's bones. He repaired the Temple and reinstated the pure worship of God. He mourned and wept because of the sins of the people. He caused the nation to assemble and renew their vows and their covenant with God.

Because of all this God was pleased to make known to him, through Huldah the prophetess, that he would defer his anger, and postpone for his sake the wrath which had been determined upon that people until Josiah should have been gathered to his fathers. So that Josiah, as their king, really stood between the nation and their coming destruction, when he was suddenly cut down—slain in battle. They brought him to Jerusalem, where he died, and was buried ; " and all Judah and Jerusalem mourned for Josiah," and made great lamenta-tion over him.

But their great mourning was of a transient and evan-escent character, followed by no good results. Scarcely had he been laid in his sepulchre, and the funeral obsequies ceased, before the reforms which he had instituted disappeared. The people relapsed into their idolatry and wickedness, growing worse and worse. In the language of the inspired writer, "They mocked the messengers of God, and despised his words, and misused his prophets, until the wrath of the Lord arose against his people till there was no remedy." In a little more than twenty years, notwithstanding their great mourning for this good king, Josiah, their sins had reached a point which could be endured no longer. By one sweep of destruction their land was made desolate, and the remnant of the people who escaped the sword were borne away into captivity. Thus we see there was, indeed, great occasion for mourning, and all Judah and Jerusalem did mourn, but their mourning was not such as tended to any permanently good results.

With a view, then, to a more abiding impression, and a more lasting improvement of this afflictive dispensation of Providence, let us proceed to notice the occasion which we as a nation this day have to mourn, and some of the lessons which this bereavement should teach us.

1st. There is occasion for mourning because it is the executive head of the nation—the representative of the law and of the authority of the Government, who has fallen. The inquiry might arise, perhaps, in the minds of some who have not duly considered the subject, What was Abraham Lincoln more than others, that a whole nation should mourn his death? I answer, simply in himself, in his own person as a citizen of our common country, he was no more than thousands of others ; but in his official capacity he was more than others, and more than others to every inhabitant of the land. Why is the American flag more to us than any other similar product of the loom? Not because of the richness of its texture or the costliness of the fabric of which it is made, but because throughout the world it is the chosen emblem of the nation's sovereignty and independence, and at home it is the representative of the nation's authority. To vindicate its honor, and to maintain its supremacy, whether at home or abroad, every patriot is ready, if need to be, to lay down his life and his fortune. So with him who for the time was chosen to rule over us as our chief magistrate, he represented the majesty of the law and the authority of the nation. In the providence of God, and by the will of the nation, expressed in strict accordance with all the forms of constitutional law, he was called out from the multitude of his equals, constituted the head of the Government, and clothed with the nation's authority and power. He was the embodiment of the nation's majesty, for its government and for its protection. Since human governments began on earth, if there ever was a man lawfully and rightfully constituted a ruler over men, he was rightfully and lawfully the chief ruler in this land. The highest were justly amenable to his executive authority ; the lowest had a claim upon him for protection ; and all had a right to demand of him that the integrity of the Government and the authority of law be maintained. In his official capacity, he stood in a different relation to every one of us from that which he occupied before, and in a different relation from that of any other man for the time. By the nation's act he was taken out from the general relation of a simple citizen of a common country and placed in a personal relation to every one of us as our ruler. All the reverence and obedience which by laws, human and divine, are due to human rulers any where, were due to him, not merely as Abraham Lincoln but as the representative of the nation's authority. All the loyalty and allegiance which are due to human governments any where were due to this Government, as embodied and represented in his official person.

Human government is not a thing in the abstract. If it exists as a reality, it must exist as represented in living men, placed in a position to wield its power and give it efficiency. The idea of law or government unrepresented in men, not embodied in particular persons charged with the exercise of the functions of such government, is a mere theory. Allegiance or loyalty to a mere abstract theory is an impossibility. If a man, therefore, will be loyal, he must be loyal to the government as represented in the persons of those who are its regularly constitued rulers. When, therefore, we did homage to him in life, it was not merely to him as Abraham Lincoln, but to him as the nation's representative. When we honor him in death, it is not as a citizen of the State of Illinois, nor as a citizen of the United States of America, but as the President of the United States—the man who wielded the power, and embodied in his person the majesty and the authority of a great and free people. There is not an inhabitant of this broad land that ought not, nor is there a loyal and right-minded one that does not, feel in his death an individual affliction, a personal bereavement. God in his afflictive providence has come near to every one of us. He has laid his hand on a

point which touches each member of the nation, and we ought
to feel it. He has spoken in tones that should vibrate in every
heart.

In the eye of divine law there is something sacred in the
person of a ruler, not merely in the office but in the person of
him to whom the office inheres. He is the minister of God,
ordained of him ; a revenger to execute wrath upon him that
doth evil ; and in the death of such an one there is a marked
and special providence to every individual of the nation. Nor
is the obligation to regard it to be evaded by the consideration
that the office and the prerogative is readily transmitted to
another equally competent and worthy. You might as well
say a man is excused from mourning on account of the death
of his wife, or is under no obligation to consider the chastisement of God upon his house in such death, because it is possible for him to obtain another wife equally good. What I
insist upon is, that this is a national bereavement. In permitting this blow to fall upon the head of the nation, God has
caused his judgment to rest upon the nation, and upon every
individual of it. And it becomes all of us to mourn, and to
humble ourselves before him in penitent sorrow.

I dwell upon this the more because in our heated party controversies we have not always suitably regarded the sacredness
of the persons of those who actually rule over us, nor the divine
sanctions which to them personally commands our loyalty,
reverence, and obedience. This is one of our sins as a nation,
and one of the principal causes of all those calamities which
have befallen us. It is, I believe, one of the lessons which
God, by his fierce judgments, is burning into the nation's conscience. Happy will it be for us if we so mourn as that the influence of this lesson shall be permanently felt in the nation's life.

2d. In this afflictive dispensation there is great occasion for mourning on account of the personal character of him who is thus suddenly stricken from the head of our national affairs. When the head of a family is removed by death, it is, and ought to be, regarded as a divine chastisement to that family— an occasion for mourning, repentance and humiliation before God ; and it adds greatly to the sense of bereavement if he was a wise, provident and good father. So when the head of a nation is smitten down, it ought to be felt to be a divine judgment, a national affliction. Especially is it an occasion for mourning if he of whom the nation be bereaved be a man possessed of those qualities of mind and heart which adapt him to the office, and to the situation of the country. It is no part of my present purpose to pronounce a penegyric on the charac- ter of him whom the nation has just honored with such extra- ordinary and unexampled obsequies, and such tokens of re- spect. Nothing in his life or history is known to me which is not equally well known to every one of you. I need not, therefore, recount his deeds. At this period of time, as we look back upon his finished career, it will not be denied that he possessed many of the qualifications of a wise and good ruler.

His intellectual abilities, certainly, were not of that showy and brilliant order which is apt to captivate the imaginations of men. He was not learned, perhaps, in all the intricacies of diplomacy nor in all the refinements of State craft. It will not be doubted, however, but that he possessed in a good degree that wisdom which goes by the more homely and less imposing name of good practical common sense, which, accompanied as it was in him, with honesty of heart and singleness of purpose, is certainly of infinitely more importance for all the just ends of government. If it is any proof of ability for a man to accomplish what one-half of the civilized world for four years strenuously affirmed never could be done—if this is any proof of ability, then certainly he has given us some proof of ability. I would not detract anything from the honor and the well-earned fame of those men who have bravely fought on the field of battle, yet surely much of the credit of calling forth and directing the resources of the nation in such manner as to bring this war to a successful and triumphant conclusion is due to him.

I am not anxious to place myself in that class of persons who are always wise after the event, and who are always ready to say, " I knew it would be so." In those times of repeated defeat and disaster on the field of battle, and of confusion and disaffection at home—in those days of darkness and national despondency, I confess to have shared the doubt whether he possessed the nerve and the mental stamina which would enable him to master the situation and control the elements with which he had to deal. He was yet, in this respect, an untried man, and the question could only be determined by the event. But looking back now upon the period of this great conflict, it must be confessed, that surrounded with difficulties as great as those which ever beset the ruler of any country, he has shown himself equal to the work which was given him to do.

I have no occasion now to discuss the principles and complicated questions involved in the controversies of political parties which led to the terrible conflict which has desolated so large a portion of our land, and carried mourning and grief into so many homes. And I might as well take this occasion to say, that in my ministry here I have refrained from all political controversy. This I have done designedly and intentionally, not from fear or favor, but from honest principle ; from a regard to the harmony, the peace, and the religious welfare of this society, from a thorough conviction that it was altogether outside of my province, and that no possible good could result from any other course. And I feel bound frankly to tell you, that if any insist upon having that kind of work done here, the sooner they get some one else to do it the better it will be for you and for me. I have now certainly no occasion to discuss the principles involved in the controversies of the past. I think I can understand how men may differ in regard to them and be honest, loyal, Christian men notwithstanding.

It will not be doubted, however, but that he whom now we mourn did represent the opinions of the majority of the nation. If any think that he was wrong in his opinions, still a man is not to be harshly judged or hastily condemned for holding sentiments which are entertained by a majority of the people of a great and free Republic. The basis of all free government being that the will of the majority shall rule, and he having been placed in a position to represent and give efficiency to that will of the majority, it must be confessed that up to the moment of his death he had borne the country through its trials with as few mistakes as we had any right to expect from any one whose wisdom was not more than human.

But one who is called to rule over a nation, especially in such times, has need of other qualifications than those of intellectual ability, and he was not deficient in them. It was the qualities of the heart rather than of the head which gave him that hold of the nation's mind which it must be acknowledged he really did possess.

In the judgment of mankind—in the sentiments of the civilized world, he stands to-day acquitted of any of that sor-

did and personal ambition which seeks individual aggrandize
ment and dominion at the expense of national liberties.
However jealous men may have been of that almost absolute
power which the necessities of the war placed into his hands
we have all lived to feel that in the whole exercise of it he was
guided by an integrity of heart, an honesty of purpose, and a
ingleness of aim, which have placed him above suspicion ; and
withal there was a frankness of manner which rendered him
incapable of duplicity—there was a genial temper and an im-
perturbable good nature which never forsook him in the most
vexatious and trying circumstances ; and a kindness of heart
to which the oppressed and the wronged never pleaded in vain.
Amid all this sea of human blood—amid all this turbulence of
human passion, and all this anguish, which has wrung the nation's heart, on his escutcheon there is not left one stain of
blood-thirstiness—there is not left the taint of one deed of dis-
honor, of wanton cruelty, or of revenge. As I look back
upon the past, as I view that conflict of opinions which, without an entire change in the moral character of the nation, rendered a conflict of arms inevitable—as I trace the progress of
the fearful strife, fraught with so many dangers to the country's future, affording just the opportunity which a Cæsar or a
Napoleon would have coveted to build an empire on the ruins
of the Republic—as I consider all this, I cannot but find occasion for devout gratitude to Almighty God that he gave us
such a man for such a time. Now when such a ruler is suddenly stricken down, every right-minded person, whatever may
be his political sentiments, cannot but feel that it is a national
calamity, a divine chastisement, an occasion for sorrow, mourning, and repentance to a whole people. I cannot resist the conviction that one of the lessons which God is teaching us by all

these terrible dealings is, that we be less bitter in our party spirit—that we be less harsh in our judgments of those who are called to rule over us, and less severe in our condemnation of those who are charged with such great and solemn responsibilities.

3d. The manner of his death is no small addition to this national bereavement, as a cause for mourning and sorrow. That such a man in such a position should be stricken down by a foul blow of murder—that he should fall by the cowardly stroke of an assassin—that our own country should produce a company of hardened wretches, capable of so infamous a conspiracy, cannot but fill the mind with horror as well as grief. When we remember too that the blow was aimed not at him personally, but at the nation's life, it not only aggravates the crime, but overwhelms the heart with mingled anguish and detestation of the deed. It was not at ABRAHAM LINCOLN that the stroke was aimed, but at the authority and life of the nation, as represented in him.

There is a sense in which his name will justly go down to posterity as a martyr to his country. According to the whole theory and foundation of all free government, the will of the majority, constitutionally expressed, is the will of the nation for all governmental purposes. No fact in human history is more clearly established than this, that he represented the will of the majority of this nation in its sovereign capacity. The will of the majority, in strict conformity with the provisions of law, was not only expressed in his first election to office, but the principles of his administration and his acts were endorsed and ratified by an increased majority in his re-election. If a majority is not to rule, then tell me who is? He was called by the sovereign voice of the people to give efficiency to the nation's will in the exercise of its high prerogative of government. He was honestly discharging that duty. Because he was honestly and faithfully executing the nation's will he was stricken down. The quarrel was not with him personally, but with the principle which he represented and which the sovereign voice of the nation decreed. The blow was aimed at the nation's life, and he, as its representative, fell the martyred victim.

In the absence of positive proof it is not for me to charge complicity with the deed upon the leaders of the rebellion. Still it is but in keeping with the attempt to destroy the unoffending inhabitants of populous cities by fire and imported pestilence. It is but in keeping with the cool, deliberate starving of thousands of disarmed prisoners of war. It was the culminating point of a most determined and relentless war upon the nation's authority. If it had been within its power, the spirit which assassinated him would have plunged the dagger into the nation's heart and poured out the nation's life-blood. That we should have fallen upon times when such a crime was possible in this free nation—when such a war could be waged against a nation's life, cannot but fill every loyal and well-disposed mind with profound gloom and mourning.

Surely one of the lessons which God is grinding into the nation's conscience, is the solemn responsibility of the American people to the government which is over them, and the respect which is due to it from them. The whole management of our political affairs has been made so much a matter of trickery and trade; so much a matter of duplicity and deception, that the people have lost in a great measure that reverential awe which the forms and enactments of just government should always inspire, and the salutary restraints which they should always impose. The whole idea of government has been lowered and degraded. The people have been educated to feel less respect for the majesty of laws and rulers than our fathers were wont to feel.

There is a solemn law of Jehovah, enacted in the interests of Eternal righteousness, and for the welfare of every nation under heaven, which reads on this wise : " Thou shalt not speak evil of the ruler of thy people." Here is at least one law of God which few American citizens comparatively seem to feel themselves bound to obey, except when the ruler happens to be of their party.

It is but a few years ago, and within the recollection of all, when many of those who now claim to be, par excellence, the loyal of the land, did not hesitate, in the pulpit and out of it, to preach resistance to the law and defiance to the powers that be. If it is treasonable and dangerous now, it was treasonable and dangerous then. The truth is, that by our political huckstering, and by our persistent habit of denouncing all our rulers indiscriminately as tyrants and knaves, we have brought our government and our rulers into contempt in the eyes of the people. And there is but one step between this state of mind and overt acts of treason. It requires but a slight occasion to call them forth. In this respect we have sown the wind and most fearfully have we been reaping the whirlwind as the consequence. There never was a truer word uttered by any ruler than that which was spoken by our present chief magistrate, when he said, "the American mind must be educated to feel that treason — resistance to government—is the greatest of crimes." Want of respect for the majesty of law and for the representatives of government, is one of the great sins of this nation. I speak not of one party, but of all parties. It is one of the great sins of this

nation—a sin which must sooner or later bring its own punish-
ment with it in the anarchy and confusion which it will inevita-
bly work in the bosom of society. My mind is deeply impress-
ed with the conviction, that one of the lessons which God, by
his judgments, is grinding into the conscience of this nation, is
a solemn reverence for constituted authority, as the representative and the delegated minister of his own divine prerogative
of executing justice on earth.

4th. The event which calls us together to-day is an occasion
for sorrow and mourning in view of the present circumstances
of the country, and the difficulties which still lie in the way of
the nation's future. I take it as no small praise to him who
has fallen, and no slight proof of his honesty and integrity of
heart, that the very people who had just been in armed rebellion against the Government, as they were compelled to yield
to rightful authority, felt that his death to them was a great
calamity. The moment forcible resistance ceased, and they
were brought powerless before the vindicated majesty of the
law, there was no man living to whose tender mercies they
would sooner have committed what remained of life and fortune than to his. And the foreign enemies of our country,
who for four years have been vilifying and denouncing him
and his administration, are now, in his uprightness of character, his kindness of heart, his answering truthfulness, his unim-
peachable sincerity, and his conciliatory spirit, able to discern
those qualifications which would eminently have fitted him to
bring about a reconciliation, and a restoration of social order.
The loss of such a man at such a time cannot but be felt by
every right-minded person to be a national calamity. The
permitting of him to be thus suddenly taken away is one of
those mysterious dispensations of Providence to which it becomes us to bow in submission but with penitent and sorrowful hearts.

Then, too, in regard to that race who by the events of the war are now released from bondage. Whatever view men may take of the complex questions involved in the controversies which preceded the rebellion, taking the situation as it now is, no man in his sober mind can think that it would be either just to them or conducive to the future peace and welfare of the country, that slavery should be reinstated. If it is not to be reinstated, then here are four millions of poor, helpless and dependent creatures, who have a claim upon us that the shield of the nation and the protection of the law shall be thrown around them. In the present state of affairs, the national government is necessarily charged with this solemn responsibility, a responsibility from which it cannot escape without proving recreant to all moral obligations. To whom then, I ask, in all this land would that race, or the nation at large, sooner have had that high and sacred trust committed, than to him whose large heart and kind disposition ever made him the friend of the oppressed.

From all these considerations, the event which calls us together to-day is an occasion for sorrow and mourning to the nation. Humanly speaking, the only thought which can reconcile us to it is, that in the eye of Infinite Wisdom, perhaps, the demands of justice and the future welfare of the Republic requires a stern work of retribution to be performed upon the guilty leaders of the rebellion, for which, by his conciliatory spirit, by his generous heart, and by his sympathetic nature, he was unfitted.

At least God is teaching us to cease to put our trust in man, but to commit all our interests, and the nation's destiny, into the hands of that just and merciful Being who ordains his own counsels, and who executes by whatever agencies it pleases him, his own eternal purposes.